'Lobsters'

Design and illustration by Patrick Fisher of Frontwards Design

Photograph by Robin Christian

 To download a free audiobook of *Lobsters*, please visit makinabooks.com/lobsters, add the audiobook to your bag and enter the code LOBSTERS at checkout

ISBN: 978-1-8384362-8-5

First published in 2021 by Makina Books • makinabooks.com

Printed in the UK by Henry Ling Limited, at the Dorset Press, Dorchester

'Lobsters'

Wayne Holloway-Smith

for Margot and Emily

[Singing]

I miss

everything

about

my life

three sticks of lipstick I ate four buttons I ate the smoke

from her red jacket a custard pot

so full of rage it torched

my tiny childhood – a heart beating against the four pillars of the room

fresh from the microwave we had discovered pain

was dielectric and lumpy – tipped into the body

from the outside o lord

did anyone ask for this type of touch

[cymbalcrash

mandolin

my heart]

and my body is a group of sudden musicians striking up a tune of longing

they don't notice our acts as living things becoming objects the radio

is getting hammered now I am singing myself

into dead stuff I ate the shadows now the shadows

are retreating imagination is a malady

this is the last time I will write about your leaving:

one life may hide another now she is gone and here I am

like Sellotape trying to hold a river in place

[a soft tuba three

perfect violins]

I'm sorry we existed like this

you woke up and were suddenly healed

to talk about the original **hunger was impossible**

your hair screwed in tight your scalp fixed to the bone

your mind banged down with **all this love** we source

our understanding of the world from our own bodies

[strings eking out

a little more

emotion

at this point

a voice two voices

singing]

how did we get down here among the potato peelings

we hold ceremonially our fingers

when "I love you" suddenly rings false when "I'm full of doubts"

hides "I'm certain about something" one of us said

I am made of hotness

one of us said and this is heart-breaking

an antibacterial wipe in the dog bowl I ate her hairspray I ate

all of the emotional music I ate monster munch right along the way to

my thirties

and we arrived knowing the whole world is happening

beneath us we're just not allowed to have much of it

it's so full on: soup in the pot broccoli hot clever water

I wanted to place a good moment on my tongue

hold several deeds closer to my skin again

I wanted to tell you something beautiful so I did

making an anchor of me

to be a person I must outgrow my own shrinking

I ate my own trainers I ate piano music then a lovely little silence

into which you emerged – like spilling water

mouthed my sad and slow-rocking song – *at the bottom of everything*

I wanted only to be useful to shout out the window at nighttime

Is everyone OK and for the world to shout back

out the window at nighttime a scurry of gerbils a street party

inside the window a creeping history of the blood

outside foxes biting the nighttime rotten

inside you are gone – walking from one room to another

out the window I literally shouted your name

is everything OK

[silence]

I ate the silence

[then a slow double bass

starting up]

one of us said eventually we have to pay the mind back

and sticking bits of my damp hair on

with spoonfuls of honey I received word

the Debenhams in Swindon had closed the chip shop in Swindon

had closed the libraries in Swindon on fire – my childhood was

shutting off its lights

[three dull drumbeats]

it feels as if I'm about to be born but can't – alone and into the present tense

if there is a god out there o wafers of Christ I am listening –

at the bottom of everything

is our drunk parents at the bottom

of everything is a piece of stained furniture

at the bottom of everything behold he comes

riding on a cloud – his muscular temper

a noise under the lights of the kitchen at the bottom

of everything is onions at the

back of my throat even then

[singing] look: I love you

I said I just need a use for this body and its music –

a destination for people to arrive at putting on

a clean smelling shirt stepping each leg

through cotton trousers and walking out

the door frame lit up and smashed

to bits by the morning –

snow in your hair snow in my eyes

and yeah one of us said here are some trees

at the bottom

of everything is

we are grown up and escapees

fireworks in the beard of god I ate

a freckle a tiny little piece of childhood: Hallelujah

I have the exact same amount of mother I always had

one of us said I got touched in the bath and it gave me an eating disorder

one of us said the earth will swallow us up and it would give me an illness –

I already have it and we spoke about the dead so much the house came down [a lit match

then the sound

of several lit matches burning]

the mornings of **the last fine days**

were the freshest – most limpid the apples

are still being ignored the crickets are screaming

bloody Tuesday and the sky everywhere

you don't seem to be happy one of us said

  oh yes I am happy but I am sad – the earth

    will swallow us but not yet

I ate all the camera angles when they circled

and it was just me

in the middle of the road with a lolly stick

from the other side

of the long city

your face appeared

inside my pocket

[an accordion

sliding

through my body]

in one dream everyone I've ever known o lord

was holding my wrists and feet

sleeves and backside so many hands

on my body thrown up then caught

and again – my stomach through the air

my chemoreceptor was butterscotch in the blood

so much love stuffed with vanilla salt

my inner-ear was corn syrup my throat filling with alkaline

and treacle thank you I am soft-cracked

and laughing myself hoarse thinking about it

[singing] look: I love you

the kindness in me is welling as if I were laying a hard-boiled egg

one of us said eventually we all have to pay the mind back

continuous and slow good pain chopping up my fringe

family I had to step over drunk to leave – look: I love you sliding from the sofa

grey carpet growing over my limbs while all the shouting keeps going –

I have locked all their names behind my jaw

one of us said let the dead bury their own dead but

what are we supposed to do with this massive shovel

I dug holes in the carpet we can sit down later and cry in

remember how much fun it was watching our fathers

bang their gums on the enamelled sink – not much:

I'm so frantic to shrug off this inheritance but

why am I running these molars around my palm

like a beaded necklace am I still carrying

so much of this Swindon – a walloping inside the guts

like a child hid inside a cutlery drawer but

ok – wow: your freckles

[one voice two voices singing]

we kicked our feelings so far out in front of us

– every so often we found one

and wrestled it backwards chased it with a stick

pinned one to the carpet of our childhoods

it's true we made several graves for the ones who were missing

when our mothers rang on Sundays we put the phones

in the ground next to the emptiness and grinned

till we became finished – at the end of the ring tones

a kiss vanishing along with its two constituent parts

you did something with your hands to something in my chest

[silence]

eventually we have to pay the mind back

what do you do when you have no positive place to land on

when the only possibility of love

in this present tense

is a karate kick one good handstand

collecting things as we go I ate

the way you smoked a cigarette

I have eaten several friendships like this

until there is nothing

[solo]:

tears sliding down my isolated chin/ **a door** clicked

outside the window our feelings

on the monkey bars our feelings on the playground

on swings building castles in the sandpit

inside the window my open shirt the open fridge

outside the window the back of you

please turn around

a dog is chasing an empty crisp packet

inside the window one toothbrush a half-finished shoe rack

I'm sorry we existed like this

from a place beneath the earth your phone not mine is ringing

Acknowledgements

I'd like to thank Out-Spoken Press and Broken Sleep Books for publishing *Lasagne* and *Colouring Book* respectively, from which some lines have been repurposed here. This poem includes moments borrowed from Kenneth Koch, Wayne Koestenbaum and Clarice Lispector, alongside echoes of Toni Morrison, Kim Hyesoon, Maggie Nelson, Roland Barthes, Lucretius and André Gide. Thanks also to Heather Phillipson for her insight, The University of Hertfordshire for an Early Career Research Fellowship, which enabled me to write this work, to Robin and Patrick of Makina Books for their love of and attention to detail and to Anthony Anaxagorou and Emily Harrison for making it OK to be in the world during an incredibly difficult time.